THE
LAND ROVER
STORY

THE
LAND ROVER
STORY

Giles Chapman

The
History
Press

Published in the United Kingdom in 2013 by
The History Press
The Mill · Brimscombe Port ·
Stroud · Gloucestershire · GL5 2QG
www.thehistorypress.co.uk

Reprinted 2014, 2016

British Library Cataloguing in Publication Data
A catalogue record for this book is available from the British
Library.

ISBN 978-0-7524-8994-0

Typesetting and origination by The History Press
Printed in Turkey by Imak.

CONTENTS

A traditional Land Rover is probably the most capable civilian vehicle you can drive on surfaces other than tarmac. There were four-wheel drive vehicles before it, and plenty of alternatives since the first Landie's low-key arrival in 1948. Some are masterfully robust and indomitable. But Land Rover Defenders – direct descendents of the very first of the breed – still trounce everything else in their ability to be custom-configured for their duties and still tackle any sort of terrain. And that's in battlefields as much as barley fields.

A Defender is a piece of pure engineering adaptable to hundreds of uses, so it's impossible for the factory to pump out

> Nothing beats a traditional Land Rover for pushing through the toughest of conditions which, in increasingly flood-prone Britain, is a real blessing!

6

▲ Remote estate land at Eastnor Castle in Herefordshire has been a Land Rover testing ground since 1961 – the prototype 129in pick-up, second from right, was the first vehicle assessed there. The others are, left to right: Range Rover Evoque, original Range Rover and a Camel Trophy 110 station wagon.

identikit versions; they're labour-intensive and a little old-fashioned to manufacture. They're not like other cars and vans. Nor are they swift or cosseting, and for these reasons the Land Rover offering has broadened into a range of entirely 'consumer' 4x4 models that are as happy belting along a motorway or cruising suburbia as they are pulling a horsebox or hacking through woodland. They're all desirable and exciting cars: Range Rover, Discovery, Freelander and, now, the Range Rover Sport and Evoque.

Land Rover has battled its way through the wilderness years of the British motor industry, outliving the innovative company that created it, to become an example of national pride. It's a British success story (despite the ultimate owners now being Indian) that's beaten back the enveloping recession with gusto. Read on to discover how it all came to be.

Did you know?

Arthur Goddard led the engineering team that developed the first Land Rover, aged just 26. Working under him were Tom Barton and Frank Shaw (transmission), Gordon Bashford (chassis), Joe Drinkwater (engine) and Sam Ostler (body design). He left the firm in 1955 but in 2010 he returned to Solihull from Australia, aged 89, as guest of honour at the Landie's 62nd birthday.

You may imagine that the humble Land Rover, probably the British vehicle the world knows best, was created by a band of heroic characters battling against the odds to keep Johnny Enemy at bay. Like the Spitfire plane, perhaps, or Bletchley Park's code-breaking computer. After all, many Land Rovers have tested their mettle in gruelling military manoeuvres, and countless rescues, humanitarian operations and explorations.

Britain's No. 1 go-anywhere vehicle, though, was born on an Anglesey smallholding and – gasp! – was initially derived from America's Jeep. That island farm belonged to Maurice Wilks, technical director of the Rover Company. Along with his managing director brother Spencer Wilks, he had since the early 1930s fashioned Rover into a profitable and greatly admired mass-market quality carmaker.

During the Second World War, Maurice Wilks scarcely had time to tend his 250 Welsh acres; Rover was frantically busy building tanks and aero engines for the

◀ Maurice Wilks, who devised the first Land Rover, and who with his brother Spencer was the guiding light behind Rover itself.

▲ It was through his mixed experiences of a war-surplus Willys Jeep similar to this one that Maurice Wilks formulated his idea for the Land Rover.

vehicle's unreliability meant it was forever returning to Rover's workshops for repairs. Spare parts were made by hand because replacements could only be bought in bulk from the USA, and by early 1947 keeping the Jeep going was getting tiresome.

Wilks couldn't buy an alternative because there simply wasn't one. Suddenly, about Easter 1947, the penny dropped: Rover should build its own. Surely there would be farmers everywhere, like Maurice, who'd appreciate a similar but much improved vehicle? Legend has it the Wilks brothers drew their first concept sketches in the sand of a Welsh beach.

There was further impetus. Building traditional cars in the post-war period was a problematic undertaking. Because of Rover's lucrative wartime Government contracts, its highly skilled workforce inhabited a superb new factory at Solihull but the quandary was what exactly to produce

Government. So he began to restore order after 1945, and bought a battered, war-surplus Jeep to help. Its four-wheel drive was brilliant for plugging through muddy fields and hauling hay bales. But the

in it. Rover had its neat M-type economy car prototype – ideal for austere, post-war Britain – but the Wilks brothers realised that, besides high tooling costs, it wouldn't suit Commonwealth countries with coarse road surfaces and vast journey distances. This was crucial because Whitehall would only sanction raw steel supplies to carmakers demonstrating a cogent export strategy; the whole emphasis was on earning foreign currency to rebuild the nation's depleted coffers after the exhausting war effort.

Rover's traditional pre-war saloon cars could easily be built again at an annual capacity of 15,000. Unfortunately, Ministry bureaucrats would only initially permit enough steel to make about 1,100. And the returns from such a meagre number wouldn't cover the cost of making them. So the Wilkses decided to press ahead with their 'farmer-friendly' vehicle as a stopgap until steel restrictions eased.

Did you know?
Land Rover, being a brand name, was initially banned from BBC radio and television mentions. If a Land Rover was reported on a battlefield or royal parade, it could only be referred to as a 'field car'; from the 1970s, however, the rule was relaxed, as there was nothing else quite like a Land Rover.

Thanks to close working experience of the defence industry, they knew almost unlimited war-surplus, aircraft-grade aluminium was readily available. This would be ideal for the bodywork of a basic vehicle and circumvent the steel 'issue'. A simple design would allow a simple production line, making most use of peoples' skills and minimising new factory installations. And they suspected their 'Land Rover' would surely generate some export business of its own anyway. The company's strategy was audacious, little more than a hunch. But the Wilks brothers were shrewd operators, lateral thinkers, and ardent manufacturers.

➤ This is a 1947 Rover 60 six-light saloon, from whose trusty 1.6-litre engine the early Land Rover would draw its motive power.

At a company board meeting in September 1947, the new machine was presented to fellow directors as 'an all-purpose vehicle on the lines of the Willys-Overland post-war Jeep', for indeed, since July 1945, the Americans had been selling the Jeep to civilians as the CJ2A Universal. The motion to produce it was carried unanimously.

Willys-Overland might have been justly annoyed at how closely Rover's earliest working prototype, running by summer 1947, drew on Jeep designs. For one thing, they shared an 80-inch wheelbase because a Jeep chassis frame was used, along with front and rear axles. The rather weedy engine was a 1389cc four-cylinder unit from the Rover 10. But its unusual central seating position hinted at its strictly agricultural bias.

This was going to be a pick-up crossed with a tractor. 'It must be much more versatile [than the Willys], more useful as a power source . . . to have power take-offs everywhere . . . be able to do everything,' Maurice Wilks instructed his engineers.

▼ The earliest prototype, photographed inside the Rover Company's workshops in Solihull, and betraying its Jeep-derived origins.

▲ Here the prototype is undergoing tests in the real world of a farmer's field, complete with plough; it was intended the vehicle could perform all manner of agricultural duties.

▲ In this view of the prototype, the central steering wheel and driving position are obvious, demonstrating Rover's thinking that it would be a tractor/ pick-up hybrid.

The 'Centre Steer' certainly earned its spurs in testing. Its power take-off drives at the front, from the engine, and at the centre and rear, from the gearbox, meant it could motorise all kinds of farm machinery, while the four-wheel drive system gave it gutsy traction and pulling power for tasks such as ploughing.

However, as Rover's quest for ultimate versatility intensified, the prototype – then basically just a Rover-powered Jeep – evolved radically. The engine was swapped for the four-cylinder, 1595cc flat-head unit from the Rover 60 saloon, providing improved torque. The four-speed gearbox and back axle came from that car too. To take power to the front axle, Rover used its pre-war speciality of an over-run freewheel, incorporating it into a special low/high range transfer case. This provided permanent four-wheel drive without a centre differential, the front axle disengaging from the manual transmission on the overrun so the front wheels could revolve faster than the rears, while a simple ring-pull mechanism in the driver's footwell allowed the freewheel to be locked for traditional four-wheel drive. This meant downhill engine braking worked only through the rear wheels.

The Land Rover proved more user-friendly, and simpler to engineer, without its tractor-like central steering wheel, so a conventional offset arrangement was adopted. Next, the bodywork was rethought to make it easier to manufacture. All panels would be hand-formed on simple tools, using sheets of 'Birmabright' aluminium-magnesium alloy. That meant the prototype's graceful

front mudguards became little more then straight-edged metal boxes. Galvanised steel components were restricted to the separate, box-section chassis frame, the bulkhead, and reinforcements for rear bodywork and doors.

The only major component Rover needed to tool-up for was the bespoke transfer case. Although the Jeep's 80-inch wheelbase remained, not a single Willys Jeep part was

▲ The over-run freewheel in the earliest four-wheel drive transmission did lead to a slight lack of coordination of axles when going downhill, but the vehicle's off-road performance was, for the time, little short of amazing.

15

used. Ironic, then, that a picture of the prototype chassis showing Jeep suspension and axles was accidentally printed in the first sales brochure . . .

Astonishingly, all this was achieved between September 1947 and the Land Rover's public debut at the Amsterdam Motor Show on 30 April 1948. Four more months elapsed before series production began at Solihull in August. But that still meant Rover had created a world-changing new class of vehicle in under 18 months.

◄ A superb example of one of the pilot-build test batch of Land Rovers, built in 1947, complete with the hood and spare wheel that did indeed become standard equipment.

The Land Rover debut dominated the Dutch exhibition, with great hubbub surrounding the Regular model's low £450 price; no Purchase Tax was payable because, legally, it was a commercial vehicle, not a car. It was extremely basic, an open-top pick-up for which such necessities as spare tyre, starting handle, and even doors cost extra. Only with the Deluxe spec would you get a one-piece padded seat backrest instead of three separate spade-shaped cushions, doors, and a draughty canvas cab with opening rear curtain.

With a 50bhp engine and a healthy 80lb/ft of torque at 2000rpm, the 22cwt Land Rover was quite a goer, bounding up slippery hills on its Avon Trackgrip tyres adorning split-rim wheels. Excellent wheel articulation thanks to tough leaf-spring suspension and limber approach/departure angles of 45/35 degrees were real advantages. On descent, it was still superbly capable, but not quite so surefooted, with its front and rear wheel speeds uncoordinated. Pulling power mattered, not acceleration, so the tardy 0–40mph time of 18 seconds was unimportant. Then again, despite weighing more than the Willys Jeep, it was faster (and wider, yet slightly shorter) and offered 24mpg; something thrifty farmers would applaud.

The Amsterdam show vehicles were among 48 pilot-production Land Rovers,

Did you know?
Of the 196,444 Series Is (plus about 85 prototype and pre-production models) made, some 70 per cent were exported.

A Series I pick-up with production green paintwork, its windscreen folded flat and the trio of shovel-shaped seatbacks that denote it as a post-1950 example.

Did you know?

In 1968, Britain's elite Special Air Service (SAS) took delivery of 72 special Land Rovers shorn of everything non-essential and given four fuel tanks for long-distance desert sorties. They were painted a specific light pink for camouflage reasons, giving rise to the 'Pink Panther' nickname.

all painted a light grey-green, built prior to the vehicle going on sale in July 1948. The actual price was a more realistic £540 and the finalised basic specification *did* now sensibly include a spare wheel, doors, starting handle and rudimentary weather protection. This was partly offset by offering one standard paint colour: Avro Anson 'cockpit green'. This was more Army-surplus material that, eventually, was used on the chassis too, previously painted silver. It was make-do-and-mend but, of course, was discreetly colour-coordinated to the British countryside!

Maurice and Spencer Wilks were gladdened by the warm reception their Land Rover initially received. The tweedy set nodded enthusiastic approval at its British debut, the 1948 Bath & West Agricultural Show. They liked its purposefulness, rust-free panels, and the fact you could run a shaft from the gearbox

Did you know?

The first British Army Land Rovers were a batch of 1,878 vehicles ordered by the Ministry of War in May 1949, but not until 1957 was it adopted as the military's standard lightweight four-wheel drive vehicle, replacing the heavy and complex Austin Champ.

to power, say, a circular saw. The 1948 Land Rover Mobile Welder kit, for example, was Rover's earliest special-purpose iteration. The Wilkses reckoned they'd come up with a no-nonsense workhorse for rural communities, and calculated Rover would probably shift 50 a week.

But the brothers were soon dumbfounded; the trickle of early orders rapidly became a

torrent. In the financial year 1948/49, Rover sold 8,000 Land Rovers against a projection of 5,000. By 1950/51, that had doubled to over 16,000 and Land Rovers outsold Rover cars such as the brand new P4 saloon by two to one. This simply was not supposed to happen. The Land Rover was intended as a temporary bridge to Rover's future, but overnight it became the company's mainstay and helped Rover lure £5m in hard foreign cash to the British economy.

Dozens of other industries and services spotted the Land Rover's potential for go-anywhere ability. Farming would be just one of its roles as the vehicle was bought by police forces, electricity boards, forest rangers, building contractors and plain, simple adventurers. They were used as rescue patrol vehicles in the Mersey Tunnel. And, of course, by armies. The first Landie to see active military service with the British Army went to Korea in 1950 where the 'Rover Mk1', as they called it, first served alongside the US Army's Willys Jeep. Our boys liked its weather protection, but reckoned it needed to be altogether tougher for true tactical advantage.

◀ The Land Rover – this pilot-build Series I is owned by Land Rover today – immediately fitted in to the English countryside after its UK debut at the Bath & West Agricultural Show in 1948.

Meanwhile, back in October 1948, Rover was readying a bold new version that proved a fascinating ancestor of today's luxury SUVs: a seven-seater Land Rover Station Wagon. Anything but utilitarian inside, the ash-framed, aluminium body was built by upmarket coachbuilder Tickford. The £959 Station Wagon had – all as standard – leather seats, a heater and a single-piece laminated windscreen, and four rear, side-facing seats that could be folded for extra luggage capacity. While regular Land Rovers had their spare wheels exposed on the bonnet, the Station Wagon hid its modesty with a discreet steel cover.

It deserved to be a success but, in Britain, there was a major bummer – it was too expensive. Because it was classed as a passenger car, it attracted Purchase Tax (a whopping £209 of the price). Only 641 were sold up to 1951, and all but 50 were exported. Survivors today are highly prized. It was the wrong car for the times but the thinking was spot-on.

Rover was initially reluctant to sink more cash into its Land Rover venture but, with sales storming ahead, the tight-knit engineering team led by deputy

▼ A left-hand drive Series I 80in prototype; of the almost 200,000 Series I production vehicles eventually built, over 70 per cent were exported.

Did you know?

Possibly the most radical Solihull-inspired military design was the Laird Centaur – an incredible half-tracked hybrid featuring the front end of a Land Rover and a tracked rear section derived from an Alvis Scorpion tank. Eight prototypes were built between 1978 and 1984, and it proved very fast over rough battlefield ground, but a lack of orders put paid to its fortunes.

chief engineer Robert Boyle soon got the approval to upgrade it. The main aim was to resolve compromises in the four-wheel drive transmission. This was achieved by ditching the freewheel device and adding an ingeniously simple dog-leg clutch, so that four-wheel drive was now selectable; in high-ratio range for road use, the Land Rover could be driven in two- or four-wheel drive, but four-wheel drive now engaged automatically when the low range was chosen. Four-wheel engine braking had arrived! This mechanism would be used on all subsequent 'Series' Land Rovers.

The selectable 4x4 system was ready for 1950 models, identifiable by headlights no

▲ There were no computers on which to test theories in 1948, so Rover engineers physically checked their Land Rover could keep plugging ahead even at a 30-degree sideways tilt.

23

24

longer covered by the mesh grille; buyers probably assumed they'd been positioned there originally to protect them from flying stones . . . when actually Rover did it to mask the cheapness and minimal chrome plating of the items! There was a metal van top option, offered painted cream to contrast with the green bodywork. And the seats were redesigned to be more shovel-than spade-shaped.

By the end of the following year, the Land Rover gained even more strength. The really big news was an engine upgrade to 1997cc. It was known as a 'Siamese bore' design because there were no water passages between the pistons. In sheer power output, there wasn't much to shout about, a mere 2bhp extra. But there was now 110lb/ft of torque at 1500rpm for stump-pulling duties, and 0–40mph acceleration in about 14 seconds. Fuel consumption, at around 21mpg, was

Did you know?

Until 1983, a hyphen appeared between 'Land' and 'Rover' only on the vehicle badges themselves, and nowhere else. This anomaly was corrected with the launch of the 110.

heavier. There was a stronger gearbox to handle the added power, and the chassis frame was substantially beefed up. Visible improvements were sidelights moved from just below the windscreen to the front wings, proper exterior door handles, and an inverted-T-shaped radiator grille.

In British Army nomenclature, this was the 'Rover Mk2', but Land Rover controversy at the time actually centred on a thorny

◀ Coachbuilder Tickford hand-made the comfortable bodywork for the first 80in station wagon, but its status as a 'car' made it too expensive for most, and there were few takers. It's very rare today.

civilian problem. At issue was the vehicle's legal status.

You could buy a Land Rover free of Purchase Tax because it was a commercial vehicle, but bundled up with that 'bargain' offer was the stipulation that, like all trucks, it was limited to 30mph on the roads. In the early 1950s, one owner appealed to the House of Lords after being fined for busting this speed limit, and the resulting kerfuffle allowed those Land Rovers not being used exclusively for trade purposes to be classified 'multi-purpose vehicles' and subject to a 60mph legal top speed limit. This was another fascinating factor in the Land Rover becoming ever more of a car and ever less of a tractor.

The first 80in Land Rover was exported to the US in 1949, where it singularly failed to catch on against its nemesis, the Willys Jeep. But the Land Rover's design simplicity and underlying ease of low-tech manufacture made export of kit-form vehicles for local assembly a great business for Rover. The company also signed deals that saw it go into licensed-manufacture with Minerva in Antwerp between 1952 and 1954, to meet a large order from the Belgian Army (oddly, these were steel-bodied and mostly two-wheel drive). There was a similar co-production with Tempo in Germany in 1953, that batch assigned to West German Border Police duties; and another with Santana in Madrid, Spain, in 1956 to cover southern Europe. Meanwhile the factory's new policy, from 1952, of contracting out versions like fire tenders to specialist converters reflected the soaring production numbers at Solihull – bursting at the seams just to meet demand for regular models.

◄ Winston Churchill was presented with this Series I on his 80th birthday, modified to accommodate the tools of a favourite hobby on his Chartwell estate – bricklaying!

ROVER

One of Britain's Fine Cars

◀ Thanks to the Land Rover's success, Rover was able to rejoin the modern car world in 1949, with the launch of the well-liked and long-lived P4 series.

◀◀ Here the coachbuilt Land Rover is in its element, picking up weekend visitors to the country – perhaps on a shooting break – from a branch line station.

The next major phase for Land Rover arrived in autumn 1953 when one of the few facets that exasperated owners – cramped rear cargo space – was addressed. This was achieved by enlarging the wheelbase to 86in (Army chiefs referred to it as the 'Rover Mk3'), with all the increase given to the back section. A dramatically elongated pick-up model was launched too, with a 107in wheelbase. Both came

with engines now modified with water channels between all their cylinders (to cure overheating problems), a new instrument panel, and neatly recessed door handles.

Rover workers celebrated building their 100,000th Land Rover in August 1954. Landie sales had long ago outpaced those of Rover cars as the tail began wagging the dog. This was also the year Land Rover revisited station wagons. The new 86in short-wheelbase three-door estate was factory-built and extremely utilitarian, its boxy body looking like it was made from giant Meccano sections. A year later, in autumn 1955, it was joined by a 107in long-wheelbase station wagon sporting five doors and ten seats. Both could be fitted with a raised 'Safari' roof; its additional outer layer of tough leathercloth-type material keeping the interior cool in baking heat and reducing condensation in winter.

▼ Land Rover's second crack at a station wagon was this strictly utilitarian affair, launched in 1954 on the 86in wheelbase chassis. Note the Safari roof on this one.

◄ Sam Shaw took this relaxed photograph of Marilyn Monroe and a Land Rover Series I in 1957 on a fashion shoot on Long Island, USA.

▲ Motorists stranded in Scotland in the 1950s are glad to see these AA patrols in their Series I Landies, as the vehicles find yet another role in British life.

➤ This terrific Land Rover print advertisement, from the mid-1950s, needed the absolute minimum of copy to get the go-anywhere message across.

Plus, an interior roof vent let in air and not rain. With cheap supplies of Army-surplus paint diminished, new colours were offered too: blue and grey.

The two new models proved highly popular. Weekly magazine *The Autocar* put its first Land Rover through the full 'Road Test' paces in March 1955. The specimen was an 86in short-wheelbase Station Wagon, and the novel four-wheel-drive concept was patiently introduced to readers. But after 315 miles of experience in this coarse and bouncy box-on-wheels, their testers declared: 'The Land Rover Station Wagon is an outstanding car that can be driven almost anywhere. The vehicle is ideally suited to towing a caravan or a horsebox, and is completely free of unnecessary frills. It is a first-rate machine.'

They caned it up the Hollinsclough motorbike trials track near Buxton, Derbyshire, and were amazed that, despite a covering of snow and plenty of small boulders, the Land Rover managed it with consummate ease, noting that, the more people aboard, the better it gripped! They

➤ The Queen and the Duke of Edinburgh in 1959 inspecting the Royal Navy's HMS *Albion* from the vantage point of a Series I specially modified for the purpose.

were impressed with its brakes; steering and cornering were judged excellent; on-road acceleration figures were found to be near-identical whether attempted in two- or four-wheel-drive (18 seconds from standstill to 50mph); and that it might just be possible to coax a top speed of 60mph from it!

➤ New for 1955 was a 107in wheelbase option which could be had with this Meccano-like ten-seater station wagon body option. Blue paintwork was now available too.

The Land Rover tested cost £893 12s 6d including Purchase Tax, with a heater £14 extra (and a radio £29 more). The glowing write-up must surely have changed hundreds of minds of readers previously dead-set on a large conventional estate car.

FACTS & DATA: LAND ROVER SERIES I

On sale: 1948–58.

Engine capacity, configuration: 1595cc & 1997cc, straight-four cylinder petrol; 2052cc, straight-four cylinder diesel.

Bodystyles: two-door, three-seater pick-up or van; two-door, seven-seater coachbuilt station wagon; three-door, seven-seater station wagon; five-door, ten-seater station wagon.

Dimensions: 3353–4407mm long, 1867mm high, 1549mm wide; wheelbase, '80-inch': 2032mm; '86-in': 2184mm; '88-inch': 2235mm; '107-inch': 2718mm; '109-inch': 2769mm.

Top speed: from 50–65mph.

Sample acceleration figures: 1595cc 80in – 0–40mph in 18 seconds; 1997cc 86in – 0–50mph in 18 seconds; 2052cc 109in diesel – 0–50mph in 28 seconds approx.

Sample prices: 80in standard in 1948 – £540; 86in station wagon in 1955 – £893; 107in station wagon in 1956 – £1,186.

Number built: 196,454.

the world's most versatile vehicle

LAND-ROVER

◀ Wonderful cover artwork from Rover's brochure for the Series IIA truly sums up the no-nonsense manliness involved in driving a Land Rover . . .

In 1956, wheelbases were increased once more, the 86in replaced by an 88in model and the 107in by a 109in, this one equipped with 'fully-floating' halfshafts. This time, the extra length went into the front end – between the front axle and the bulkhead – as Rover engineers prepared their next surprise: a diesel engine option. All decent off-roaders offer one today but, back then, small high-performance diesels were almost unknown. In the early 1950s, experiments had been undertaken by Wolverhampton's Turner Manufacturing, which fitted a Land Rover with its supercharged 2-litre, two-cylinder diesel engine. But in early June 1957, Land Rover was ready with its own, designed with help from Ricardo Consulting Engineers of Worthing.

This overhead-valve design offered 52bhp, identical to the petrol engine, and 87lb/ft of torque at 2000rpm. It allowed a top speed of just 53mph, but the payback was 35mpg fuel economy and, for many fleet customers, fuel parity with lorries and tractors.

Meanwhile, the 109in Land Rover could be had with Standard or Deluxe cab, plus the exciting new factory paint option of beige! Only long-wheelbase five-door Station Wagons remained out of step: this always kept the 107in wheelbase, and never came with diesel power; due to the

Did you know?

Land Rover, along with Leyland Trucks, was set to be sold to General Motors in 1986, but public and political fears over closures and job losses led to the deal being axed. After that, Land Rover Ltd was reintegrated into Rover Group.

demands of production capacity at Solihull, management decreed the ten-seater Station Wagon just fine as it was.

The last Series I 86in Land Rover was built in April 1958, with the final 107in Station Wagon completed four months later. For returning to the Amsterdam motor show that year, Land Rover presented the Series II.

◀ Series II Land Rovers had a pronounced waistline which allowed widened cabin accommodation; this is a 109in pick-up in full cry.

◀ The bare bones, in brochure illustration form, of a 109in Land Rover with 2.25-litre petrol engine; you can see that the petrol tank would be positioned under the driver's seat.

► In 1958 the Series II range was launched – this is the 88in utility version – and they were immediately identifiable by deeper side panels that now concealed the chassis and other parts.

►► These 88 Series IIs were built at the Land Rover factory for royal tour duties in 1959, kicking off that year with the Queen's visit to Canada. The dark claret/red coachline livery is a Buckingham Palace favourite.

None of the fundamental Land Rover virtues were altered but the body now featured deeper sides thanks to skirts below door-level to conceal the chassis and exhaust pipe. The bodywork featured a pronounced, bulging waistline that helped make the cabin less cramped. Under the bonnet was an enlarged 2.25-litre petrol engine, and three years later it was joined by a diesel version of the same unit that was much more powerful than its predecessor. At that stage in 1961, the Series II became the IIA.

Throughout the 1960s and '70s, Land Rover production escalated until it reached its annual peak in 1971 at 56,564. The 250,000th had been built in 1959, the 500,000th would roar out of Solihull in 1966, the 750,000th in 1971, and the millionth in 1976. Over that period, Rover would first merge with Leyland/Triumph and then, in 1968, become part of the ill-starred British Leyland. That meant it was also a part of the corporation bailed out by the Government and effectively nationalised in 1975. However, the Land Rover operation stood apart, doing its own thing and enjoying a high degree of

▼ This picture largely speaks for itself. This is but a tiny fraction of the Land Rover Series IIs exported, most fully built like this but many as kits for local assembly.

model on the 109in wheelbase. It was strictly a commercial vehicle, with the cab squeezed up and above the engine to allow maximum space for the rear bodywork – either a factory-built pick-up or else anything bespoke the customer commissioned. Its four-wheel drive workhorse credentials were outstanding, gutless though it was until 1966 when Rover's six-cylinder 2.6-litre engine from the old P4 saloon gave a new 110in wheelbase Series IIB version

◄ Another brochure picture that shows how the 88in model was configured to take seven people in station wagon form.

▼ The Forward Control Land Rover took its bow at the Geneva motor show in 1962, featuring a cab above the engine and a greatly increased cargo space in factory pick-up guise.

autonomy as the rest of the BL car-making operation reeled under industrial strife and some less-than-excellent new products.

The most radically different Land Rover yet seen arrived at the 1962 Geneva Motor Show, the high-riding Forward Control

some much-needed oomph. But it was never a strong seller, and was axed in 1972. Massively more worthwhile to Rover was the introduction of the Series IIA Lightweight.

British Forces had been using Land Rovers for years, generally for light, peace-keeping duties. But with the advent of the capacious Westland Wessex helicopter, there was now the opportunity to drop a vehicle weighing under 2500lb right on to the front line. Trouble was, nothing suitable existed and the Land Rover Series IIA was much too heavy and bulky to become the 'Airportable' that was required. So, working with experts at the Fighting Vehicles

◀ A 109in pick-up lends a hand to give a demonstration run of Proteus-Bluebird CN7, Donald Campbell's machine that set a world land speed record of 403.10mph at Utah in 1964.

Did you know?

In 1990, the extra-long-wheelbase 127 was renamed the 130; not that 3in were added to its already massive length . . . it was just a numerical tidying-up exercise to bring it in line with the 90 and 110.

FACTS & DATA: LAND ROVER SERIES II & IIA

On sale: 1958–71.

Engine capacity, configuration: 1997–2286cc, straight-four cylinder petrol; 2052–2286cc, straight-four cylinder diesel; 2625cc, straight-six petrol.

Bodystyles: two-door, three-seater pick-up or van; three-door, seven-seater station wagon; five-door, ten-seater station wagon; also two-door, three-seater forward control pick-up and derivatives.

Dimensions: 3617–4445mm long, 1969mm high, 1676mm wide; wheelbase, '88-inch': 2235mm; '109-inch': 2769mm.

Top speed: from 50–75mph.

Sample acceleration figure: 2286cc petrol IIA 88in – 0–50mph in 16 seconds.

Sample price: IIA 109in station wagon in 1970 – £1,019.

Number built: Series II – 126,000 approx; Series IIA – 451,624.

▶ Much versatility was provided by the 110in-wheelbase Forward Control chassis, leading to interesting new four-wheel drive spin-offs like this compact fire tender.

Research and Development Establishment in Chertsey, Surrey, Land Rover designed a stripped-down Lightweight Truck Utility Half-Ton. It was narrowed, the axles were shortened, a spare wheel and bumpers were omitted, and all upper bodywork, windscreen included, was flat and easily detachable. In short, and with a petrol engine, it was perfect for the job.

The Lightweight entered production in 1968 and enjoyed a fifteen-year run, eventually being bought by armed forces from twenty other countries. It was the military breakthrough Land Rover had been chasing for years, and the company was anxious to capitalise on it. Three years after the Lightweight entered its swashbuckling service, at the 1972 Commercial Vehicle Show in London, the latest Land Rover engineering masterpiece was unveiled. This was a new Forward Control, the so-called 101 1-Ton after its 101in-long wheelbase, designed solely for military use as a vehicle that could tow 4000lb artillery trailers and their ilk.

The 101 had its own purpose-designed chassis, with a 3.5-litre Rover V8 engine and matching LT95 gearbox directly

beneath the cab, and its transfer case took power to the bespoke Salisbury front and rear axles suspended by newly designed half-elliptic suspension. It was a superb, fit-for-purpose machine. Thanks to advances

▲ The Lightweight Truck Utility Half-Ton gave Land Rover the approval it had long sought from Britain's armed forces, and was in production for 15 years from 1968.

in helicopter technology, it too could be parachuted into battle, and Land Rover also created a powered trailer that could turn it into a six-wheel drive entourage – its nifty coupling system allowed the trailer to rotate through 360 degrees without losing power. The 101 was in production between 1975 and 1978 for the British and Australian armies, and was in service as an ambulance up to the late 1990s in Kosovo.

◀ This on-track demonstration of Land Rover diesel-engined muscle was staged at the launch of the IIA in 1961; factory engineers fitting special flanged wheels for the event.

Scottish engineering company Cuthbertson came up with this tracked Land Rover conversion for truly the most uneven of terrain, and it proved invaluable to bomb-disposal teams.

So much for Land Rovers as fighting vehicles, but what of their ongoing appeal on Civvy Street? Well, the Series IIA was well suited, or adaptable, to virtually any customer requirement throughout the early 1960s. From some quarters came a call for more power, leading Rover to offer its 2.6-litre six-cylinder engine as an option, and for those needing a high-capacity truck there was a burly pick-up

This Series IIA 109 pick-up had a major job on its hands – even if it had the bigger 2.6-litre six-cylinder engine – to haul this 'gooseneck' trailer and its cargo of a four-wheel drive Roadless tractor.

This diverse group of mostly Series IIA vehicles shows the enormous variety of applications that Land Rovers could be put to; notice the relative paucity of Forward Control models.

▲ There were many improvements in the Series III Land Rover that took its bow in 1971, although purists were none too impressed by the fitment of – gasp – a *plastic* radiator grille.

with a 1-ton payload. Finally, in 1968, the headlights were moved out from the grille and into the front wings – a worthwhile change that made it easier to gauge how close an approaching Land Rover really was at night!

Outsiders wouldn't have realised but development of the basic Land Rover slowed

to a trickle in the late 1960s as all effort was poured into the launch of the radical new Range Rover (*see pages 54–5*). Nonetheless, in 1971, the third-generation Land Rover range arrived, mildly updated from the Series II. Diehards were a mite scornful of the plastic grille and headlight surrounds, but the new fascia was a great improvement.

▲ A useful fleet order for Land Rover in around 1976 was this consignment of a dozen 88in Station Wagons for HM Coastguard.

FACTS & DATA: LAND ROVER SERIES III

On sale: 1971–85.

Engine capacity, configuration: 2286cc, straight-four cylinder petrol; 2286cc, straight-four cylinder diesel; 2625cc straight-six petrol; 3528cc, V8 petrol.

Bodystyles: two-door, three-seater pick-up, high-capacity pick-up or van; three-door, seven-seater station wagon; five-door, ten-seater station wagon.

Dimensions: 3617–4480mm long, 1969mm high, 1676–1680mm wide; wheelbase, '88-inch': 2235mm; '109-inch': 2769mm.

Top speed: from 66–80mph.

Sample acceleration figures: 2286cc petrol 88in – 0–50mph in 16 seconds; 3528cc V8 petrol 109in station wagon – 0–60mph in 26.1 seconds.

Sample prices: 88in station wagon in 1973 – £1,115; 109in V8 pick-up in 1981 – £5,733.

Number built: 541,156.

THE RANGE ROVER

It was the liking for rugged vehicles like the Jeep Wagoneer, Chevrolet Blazer and Ford Bronco by well-off, active American families that alerted Rover to the possibilities of a proper, sophisticated, dual-purpose 'lifestyle' Land Rover. Work began in earnest in 1966 on what was known at first as the '100-inch Station Wagon'.

The natural powerplant was the all-aluminium former-Buick 3.5-litre V8 engine, an asset Rover had cannily bought from General Motors, allied to a permanent four-wheel drive system. But instead of the Land Rover's bone-shaking 'cart' springs a new chassis featured long-travel coil spring suspension. Four-wheel dual-circuit disc brakes and a collapsible steering column were notable safety features.

'The idea was to combine the comfort and on-road ability of a Rover saloon with the off-road ability of a Land Rover. Nobody was doing it at the time,' recalled Charles Spencer 'Spen' King, chief engineer, project driving force . . . and nephew of Land Rover instigator Maurice Wilks.

Engineer Gordon Bashford mapped out the vehicle's proportions and it was masterfully finessed by designer David Bache to give the crisp, starched look that would become the Range Rover's unmistakable trademark. Another stylist, Tony Poole, came up with the name: Range Rover. Like all Land Rovers up until then, the panels were aluminium.

A beautifully preserved example of the original Range Rover photographed in Snowdonia where, incidentally, the pictures for the car's original brochure were shot.

Launched in Cornwall on 17 June 1970, the Range Rover was an immediate hit, a comfortable rather than overtly luxurious car. Early unease among Rover's sales team soon lifted as the Range Rover became a must-have for wealthy types with a love for the great outdoors.

Roger Crathorne, today Land Rover's heritage guru, was one of the Range Rover development engineers, and recalls being amazed when he first drove one at 100mph on the MIRA test track at Nuneaton. But he was even more bowled over by its off-road prowess – much better than any contemporary Land Rover.

'The reason was axle articulation, on account of those coil springs. It had double the articulation of a normal Land Rover and, as a result, was more comfortable and more capable over rough terrain.' The early cars were fairly basic inside, with moulded plastic upholstery and rubber flooring so they could, if necessary, be hosed out! Although carpet sections were soon added to the boot and around the transmission tunnel (which aided sound-proofing), it wasn't until 1980 that the interior began to get opulent, only in 1981 did a four-door option arrive, and there was no auto until 1982. It took seventeen years to reach the USA, as it failed to comply with constantly shifting safety and emission rules, but when it did very belatedly arrive – the cabin trimmed in leather and wood – in 1987 it was massively popular.

The car was in production, basically unaltered, until 1995, and 317,615 were sold.

Did you know?

The first and only factory-built automatic 'traditional' Land Rover sold in the UK was the 1998 Defender 50th edition. It also came with air-conditioning. Just 385 were sold here, and it was the last V8-engined Defender.

▲ Land Rovers have long been a favourite for conversion to ambulance use. This is a IIA clearly bound for duties abroad, if the left-hand drive is anything to go by.

Also, the arrival of synchromesh on all four gears and more powerful brakes made driving a Series III less of a battle.

And that, really, was that for the remainder of the 1970s. Unlike other parts of British Leyland, the Land Rover wasn't broken, so it didn't need fixing.

▲ Introduced in 1972 and powered by the Range Rover's mighty V8, the brawny 101 1-Ton could be ordered with a powered trailer, making it a formidable six-wheel drive military combo.

▲ The Lightweight was also upgraded to Series III spec, with headlights moved from grille to front of wings. It could be parachuted on to a battlefield from a transport plane, using special airbags to cushion its landing.

In fact, the vehicles were so consistently popular and profitable, and the Solihull operation so largely self-contained that, in 1978, it became a separate entity as 'Land Rover Limited' was formed by feisty BL boss Michael Edwardes – severing it from the Rover car operation for the first time. The new autonomy came with a £200m budget for investment that company bosses called 'Stage 1', leading to an interesting new vehicle in 1979 that also, unofficially, carried the Stage 1 title.

This was a powerful new version of the 109in long-wheelbase Land Rover fitted with the 3.5-litre V8 engine and LT95 four-speed gearbox from the hugely popular Range Rover. This one, like the Rangie, had permanent four-wheel drive. In pick-up,

▼ Throughout the 1970s and early '80s the Series III sailed on virtually unchanged, and above the general morass of British Leyland. This is a very late-model SIII Station Wagon with Safari roof.

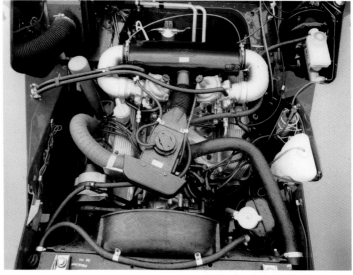

◀ An AA patrol Series III 88in vehicle attends a washed-up Ford in a ford; the picture was taken in about 1984.

▲ A V8 engine arrived as an option in Land Rovers in 1979. The model was known internally as the Stage 1, and is seen here being put through its off-road paces in Safari-topped Station Wagon form.

▲ The Stage 1 V8 engine installation was a tight squeeze, and meant the grille had to be extended forwards to be flush with the front wings.

Did you know?
The three millionth Land Rover vehicle was a
Freelander V6, built in 2001 and destined for the North
American market.

van, station wagon or bare chassis forms it was ready for all sorts of high-performance roles with emergency services and the like as the V8 engine – despite being detuned (so the Land Rover's antediluvian brakes and suspension could cope with the extra pressures put on them) to 91bhp from the Range Rover's 135 – allowed an 80mph top speed and much more rapid acceleration. A fantastic amount of torque, or pulling power, was now on tap too.

You could spot a V8 model instantly because the grille was moved forward to be flush with the front wings, to accommodate the new powertrain.

As ever at Land Rover in this period, evolution was slow and cautious because

◄ The Stage 1 V8 used the 3.5-litre engine from the Range Rover but detuned from 135bhp to 91bhp, so it wouldn't overload the Land Rover's brakes and steering. This is the pick-up version, Britain's beefy response to Japan's Toyota Hilux 4x4.

◀ The Cou[...] arrived for 'S[...] Rovers in 19[...] better seats, [...] and some n[...] stripes.

Did you know?
The Conran Design Group was closely involved in creating the interior of the original Discovery. Although some of its cuter ideas, such as a sunglasses case in the steering wheel centre, were vetoed by Land Rover, the car won a British Design Award in 1989.

customers valued and understood Land Rover's proven capabilities. Foreign rivalry, however, was hotting up. The Stage 1 V8 option came about partly to combat powerful and nimble four-wheel drive pick-ups typified by the terrific Toyota Hilux, as well as the impressive new Mercedes-Benz G-Wagen. This intensifying competition started to focus Land Rover on the bone-jarring ride and minimal comfort of its vehicles, and engineers began to experiment with hybrids that united the smoother and more forgiving coil-spring

RANGE ROVER K75 YKV Tdi

▲ During the 1980s, the Range Rover went determinedly upmarket, with automatic transmission, opulent Vogue interior and four doors. This is the 1992 Tdi model.

suspension of the Range Rover with the Land Rover chassis. It was not before time, as the 1980s would prove.

By 1982, Rover car production relocated to Cowley, giving over the entire Soilhull plant to Land Rover's activities. The company, separately, had also taken on the old British Leyland Sherpa van-making operation nearby; it was renamed Freight Rover to try to rub off a little magic on the humble vans, and some new vehicles were designed, but it was never a neat fit with Land Rover, and in 1987 company overlords transferred it to Leyland Trucks.

▲ This ghosted image of the 1983 110, in station wagon form, clearly shows the vastly more comfortable coil-spring suspension system derived from that in the Range Rover.

➤ Land Rover 110s are carefully pieced together, largely by hand, on the production line at Solihull near Birmingham, in 1983.

The 110 joined its predecessors as an essential tool for Britain's emergency services, such as police patrols as here, with its innate ability to cope with any situation.

A hydraulic platform has been added to this 110 chassis operating in 1980s Switzerland, together with fold-out stabiliser legs to keep working at height a safe occupation.

FACTS & DATA: LAND ROVER 90, 110 & 127

On sale: 1983–90.

Engine capacity, configuration: 2286–2495cc, straight-four cylinder petrol; 2286–2495cc, straight-four cylinder diesel/turbodiesel; 3528cc, V8 petrol.

Bodystyles: two-door, three-seater pick-up, high-capacity pick-up or van; three-door, seven-seater station wagon; five-door, ten-seater station wagon, four-door long-wheelbase utility.

Dimensions: 4077–5130mm long, 2037–2134mm high, 1791mm wide; wheelbase, '90-inch': 2362mm; '110-inch': 2800mm; '127-inch': 3226mm.

Top speed: from 66–86mph.

Sample acceleration figures: 2495cc diesel 110 station wagon – 0–60mph in 29 seconds; 3528cc V8 petrol 90in station wagon – 0–60mph in 14.7 seconds.

Sample prices: 110 2.2 petrol station wagon in 1984 – £6,700; 90 2.5 petrol station wagon in 1989 – £12,493.

Number built: 160,000 approx.

Likewise, a joint-venture with Carbodies to share the Range Rover as the basis for a new London taxi was abandoned.

The ever-swelling popularity of the Range Rover had convinced incoming boss Tony Gilroy that a prosperous future was not to be had from churning out rough-and-ready industrial vehicles. As if to prove the point, the Isuzu Trooper arrived in 1981, the Mitsubishi Pajero/Shogun in 1982, and there were accomplished updates of the Datsun Patrol and Toyota Land Cruiser. All of them were high-riding, four-wheel drive off-roaders in the form of comfortable estate cars. They were all cheaper than a Range Rover. And all of them could match a Land Rover station wagon for everything but the most demanding functions.

➤ The Mitsubishi Pajero (or Shogun, as it was called for UK customers) doesn't seem terribly noteworthy today, but it helped bring Range Rover-style sport-utility motoring to a much wider circle of car buyers.

➤➤ A military ambulance based on a Land Rover first entered service with the RAF in 1954. So the XD 130 model of 1997 continued a long tradition. The bodywork contract went to Marshall of Cambridge.

◀ When the Humber Bridge opened in 1981, it was the world's longest single-span suspension bridge, and these two Land Rover Series III 109s were procured to patrol it.

◀◀ A 90 pick-up with canvas tilt, circa 1987. It's amazing how, really, this vehicle was a slow-cooked version of the original Land Rover you can see on page 16.

So, as well as quickly devising a four-door Range Rover and taking its specification swiftly upmarket, Stage 1 money was poured into putting a more civilised Land Rover on sale. It arrived as the 110 and 90 (both indicating extended wheelbase inches) in 1983 and '84 respectively.

The big news, of course, was the all-round coil-spring suspension ousting the masochistic leaf-spring set-up of yore, but there was much more. Petrol or diesel engines now thankfully came with a five-speed manual gearbox for reasonably tolerable motorway. A wider track boosted stability and was obvious through new flared wheelarches in body-matching polyurethane plastic. A Series III V8-style nose was now standard, fronted by a new plastic grille, because a V8 engine (with four-speed manual gearbox) was part of the standard range for both short- and long-wheelbase Landies. Something different

again was a stretched-capacity crewcab pick-up, the 127 model of 1985, with 17in added to its wheelbase.

By Land Rover's generally glacial pace of change this was radical stuff, although the transformation wasn't completed until 1985 brought more, belated refinements. The V8 model was gifted a five-speed gearbox too, four-cylinder capacities were increased to 2.5-litre, and all models saw their crude sliding windows replaced with wind-down items.

◄ The military Defender XD, which entered British Army service in 1997 after prolonged appraisal. Although assembled on the regular Defender line, only the chassis rails and outer panels were shared, and the XD had a unique 24-volt electrical system.

Did you know?

The Discovery 3 of 2006 had a different name in US and Middle East export markets, where it was known as the LR3 – done, it is said, to distance it from the previous Discovery, which had suffered poor reliability. Non-European market Discovery 3s also came with a 4-litre V6 petrol option, the engine sourced from Ford in Germany.

The 90, 110 and 127 genuinely had a new lease of life that kept them untouchable as the best four-wheel drive workhorses you could buy. Yet the 4x4 market was booming in another sphere entirely, as Shogun, Trooper, Patrol and Land Cruiser sold in increasingly enormous numbers. Also from Japan, they were joined by the Daihatsu Fourtrak, and in the US the compact, less truck-like Ford Bronco II and Chevrolet S10 Blazer led the new compact 'sport-utility vehicle' (SUV) market.

These cars weren't being bought by farmers and construction workers but by ordinary suburban families with active lifestyles and the occasional need to drive

➤ Discovery's arrival in 1989 belatedly brought Land Rover to the burgeoning SUV sector, the new three- and five-door cars cleverly adapting Range Rover underpinnings.

FACTS & DATA: LAND ROVER DISCOVERY I

On sale: 1989–98.

Engine capacity, configuration: 1994cc straight-four cylinder petrol; 2495cc straight-four cylinder turbodiesel; 3528–3946cc, V8 petrol.

Bodystyles: two-door, five-seater station wagon; five-door, five/seven-seater station wagon.

Dimensions: 4539mm long, 1966mm high, 1793mm wide; wheelbase 2540mm.

Top speed: from 92–106mph.

Sample acceleration figures: 2495cc Tdi five-door – 0–60mph in 17.2 seconds; 3946cc V8 five-door – 0–60mph in 10.8 seconds.

Sample prices: three-door in 1989 – £15,750; five-door 3.9 V8 in 1983 – £21,494.

Number built: 348,621.

along beaches or rough tracks, or maybe tow a boat trailer or small horsebox. After decades during which the car industry had foisted ever lower and sportier family cars on customers, adding the manly halo effect by campaigning their regular models in racing and rallying, people found they enjoyed sitting up high with a commanding

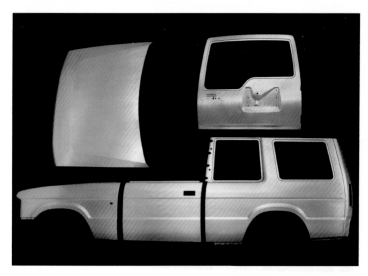

▲ Like all Land Rovers, the Discovery's body panels were made of aluminium, and here are the naked pressings that went together to form its distinctive new shape.

Jeep Cherokee. The Cherokee was the first four-wheel drive vehicle from the USA to abandon the traditional construction method of a strong, ladder-like chassis on to which a separate body structure was bolted. The traditional body-on-frame format meant the chassis structure had to be extremely heavy as it was the principal load-bearing item, and SUVs so-built – mostly derived from pick-ups used for slow-moving commercial duties – sometimes proved dangerous in the hands of former car drivers at high cruising speeds, especially those who felt the elevated driving position afforded by an SUV somehow offered them protection in accidents. Of course, it was all down to the driver, but truck-based SUVs usually had a high centre of gravity and a lot of weight to bring to a halt in an emergency. Plus, the heavy chassis construction meant old-style SUVs from Ford and General Motors (and Jeep's

view of the road. With the security of four-wheel drive at their feet, car buyers willingly forsook swift acceleration and ultimate high top speed. They felt safer in these 4x4 SUVs.

Then, in 1984, came a defining moment in global SUV evolution: the arrival of the

Although the Discovery was aimed squarely at the middle-class 'civilian' market, the emergency services were naturally interested in the versatile new car for, as here, police patrol duty.

The big leap forward in off-roader design in the 1980s came not from Land Rover but America's Jeep, the car-like road manners of the 1984 Cherokee attributable to its integral body/chassis construction.

A thrifty 2-litre four-cylinder petrol engine option in the Mpi increased the Discovery's nascent appeal to suburbia, where it didn't need huge reserves of pulling power anyway.

own, ageing Wagoneer) had a monster fuel thirst.

The Cherokee's breakthrough was its 'Uniframe' integral construction of body and chassis, making the entire welded structure of the shell bear the weight of the car. Freed of the steel girder millstone, Jeep could then give the Cherokee four doors in a compact yet satisfyingly boxy shape. A wide track meant protruding, square-rigged wheelarches. So it looked macho without actually being a brute. Its

Did you know?
The Freelander 2 TD4_e, launched in March 2009, became the world's first SUV with an intelligent stop/start system. This shuts the engine down when the vehicle stops, automatically restarting when the driver operates the clutch to engage gear, significantly cutting CO_2 emissions.

FACTS & DATA: LAND ROVER DISCOVERY II

On sale: 1998–2004.
Engine capacity, configuration: 2493cc straight-five cylinder turbodiesel; 3946–4552cc, V8 petrol.
Bodystyles: five-door, five/seven-seater station wagon.
Dimensions: 4704mm long, 1941mm high, 1890mm wide; wheelbase 2540mm.
Top speed: from 98–114mph.
Sample acceleration figures: 2493cc Td5 ES – 0–60mph in 17.1 seconds; 3946cc V8 – 0–60mph in 9.6 seconds.
Sample price: Td5 ES in 2004 – £33,095.
Number built: 300,727.

base engine was a thrifty 2.5-litre four-cylinder which, nonetheless, gave a good performance because of the then-exotic fitment of power-boosting fuel injection. And the car's roadholding was excellent. Accident rates proved the Jeep was just about as safe and as unlikely to roll over as any standard US sedan.

Its appealing compact size put Cherokees on suburban American drives like no SUV before it. In 1984, Jeep sold 154,801 vehicles but by 1989 it was up to 249,870

– the increase accounted for entirely by surging Cherokee demand.

Enough about Jeep! The point is, the market was changing swiftly and Land Rover needed to be part of the new wave or it would become a sidelined anachronism. Hence, the company's engineers and designers spent most of the mid- to late 1980s immersed in 'Project Jay'.

There simply wasn't the budget available to create a Cherokee- or Shogun-beater from scratch, so the concept focused instead on deriving an affordable family off-roader from the existing Range Rover. That meant the separate chassis would, for now, have to be retained, but the new car would receive an entirely new body with several distinctive aspects, such as the stepped roofline and body panels with crafty curvature to them – something genuinely new to Land Rover – to reduce its visual bulk.

The interior, with two optional rear-most seats in a sideways-facing position, was intended to accommodate seven people, so the spare wheel was hung outside on the side-hinged fifth door. Perhaps acknowledging that Solihull designers weren't renowned for their inviting cabins, Conran Design was called in to generate fresh thinking for the interior design. From Conran came the idea for using uplifting Sonar Blue colouring throughout,

▲ Land Rover's Special Vehicles division created a Commercial edition of the Discovery, after a healthy demand was detected among small businesses for a capable 4x4 van.

In 1990, soon after the Discovery was introduced, the trad Landies got a new name too; Defender. This is a 90 Hardtop with the new nomenclature.

as well as a zip-up storage bag for the glass sunroof panel and a portable shoulder bag nestling between the two front seats.

The radical new Land Rover was launched in 1989 under the title Discovery, the start of a new thematic naming policy created by marketing consultant Interbrand. At £15,750, it was about half the Range Rover's price, and cost the same with either the company's 2.5-litre direct-injection turbodiesel or petrol 3.5-litre V8 petrol. In 1990, a five-door joined the range.

FACTS & DATA: LAND ROVER DEFENDER

On sale: 1990–.

Engine capacity, configuration: 2198–2495cc, straight-four cylinder turbodiesel; 2493cc straight-five cylinder turbodiesel; 3528–3946cc, V8 petrol.

Bodystyles: two-door, three-seater pick-up, high-capacity pick-up or van; three-door, five/seven-seater station wagon; five-door, seven/nine-seater station wagon; four-door, six-seater utility.

Dimensions: 4077–5130mm long, 2037–2134mm high, 1791mm wide; wheelbase, '90-inch': 2362mm; '110-inch': 2800mm; '127-inch': 3226mm.

Top speed: from 85mph (Defender 90 Td5).

Sample acceleration figure: 2198cc turbodiesel 90 station wagon – 0–62mph in 14.7 seconds.

Sample prices: 90 2.5 petrol station wagon in 1993 – £15,797; 110 2.2 high-capacity pick-up in 2012 – £23,855.

Number built: 522,000 approx to end August 2012.

The Discovery fairly blew away its Japanese opposition for both image and sheer off-road prowess. The uniquely capable permanent four-wheel drive, stout separate chassis and supple springing made it unbeatable. But the original Discovery

◀ Italy never produced a credible domestic Land Rover rival, which is why they are imported and pressed into service nationwide, such as here for the national fire and rescue service.

➤ A high-capacity pick-up body has been in the Land Rover catalogue since the late 1960s, and it's seen here adorning a 2006 vintage Defender chassis.

also drove straight into Britain's suburban heartlands, establishing a Land Rover as an utterly convincing alternative to traditional large family estates.

The 1990s provided a fresh landscape for Land Rover. Like other car firms, it now made a wide range of vehicles, and that brought new issues about how to structure its offerings. So in 1990, the staple Land Rover gained its own 'textual' model name for the first time: Defender. To ensure the policy was more than superficial, this coincided with the introduction of the more flexible 200Tdi turbodiesel engine. The Discovery and Defender were upgraded with a similar but much-improved engine entitled 300Tdi in 1994, when further engine changes were made: a 2-litre petrol for the Discovery in European export markets, a 3.9-litre V8 and, for UK-market Defenders, the V8 option was axed. To get the Discovery into the lucrative US market it needed a safety upgrade to include twin airbags, leading to a total interior revamp that largely eradicated the controversial Conran touches.

Did you know?

A comprehensive revamp of 2012 Land Rovers saw a new ZF eight-speed automatic gearbox offered in the diesel Discovery, with a rotary selector and column-mounted paddles so the system can be overridden manually.

THE SECOND-GENERATION RANGE ROVER

Arriving in 1994, this was a thorough update of the original, retaining a much improved version of the old range Rover chassis but with a generally rather anonymous and – in comparison with its inspired predecessor – boring new body style.

It was known internally as the P38A simply because it was developed in building 38A at the Solihull factory.

The interior took a quantum leap forward in comfort and luxury touches, and a new BMW 2.5-litre straight-six turbodiesel was on offer beside the much-loved Rover V8 in 3.9- and 4.6-litre forms. Height-adjustable air suspension, introduced at the tail end of the MkI's life in 1992, was now standard on all P38As.

The 4.6 was the most responsive Rangie yet, reaching 60mph in 9.3 seconds, and capable of 125mph. Before production finished in 2001 there were myriad limited editions, including the all-black (David) Linley model, with just six sold, which at £100,000 was the costliest factory-offered model ever.

The second-generation Range Rover was just as capable as its forebear, but its exterior redesign somehow destroyed the angular character of the original.

Wildly successful though the Discovery was – by 1995, it helped Land Rover sell more than 100,000 vehicles annually for the very first time – the market for off-roaders was widening still. The 1989 Suzuki Vitara had ignited demand for small, compact SUVs, but the Toyota RAV4 five years later emerged as the game-changer. Although its rugged visage, large wheels and high ground-clearance impressed, underneath it was an all-wheel drive Toyota Corolla given a powerful Camry engine. So it felt very similar to a 4x4 family car to drive.

This time, Land Rover proved itself much more on the case – propelled by the ambitions of BMW, which had acquired Rover Group in 1994 – and the Freelander received much excited attention at its Frankfurt Motor Show debut in autumn 1997. Looking back, it's amazing that the project, codenamed CB40, proceeded so fast and to such thorough engineering standards.

The seed for the idea was sown at the tail end of the 1980s, with design teams from both Rover and Land Rover

▼ Toyota's original RAV4 of 1994 was a true game-changer, bringing four-wheel drive and a commanding driving position to compact cars in a no-brainer package.

FACTS & DATA: LAND ROVER FREELANDER I

On sale: 1997–2006.

Engine capacity, configuration: 1795cc, straight-four cylinder petrol; 2497cc, V6 petrol; 1994–1951cc, straight four-cylinder turbodiesel.

Bodystyles: three-door, five-seater convertible or hardtop; five-door, five-seater station wagon.

Dimensions: 4422–4448mm long, 1707–1753mm high, 1806–1808mm wide; wheelbase 2565mm.

Top speed: from 103–113mph.

Sample acceleration figures: 1795cc Softback – 0–60mph in 12.3 seconds; 2497cc five-door – 0–60mph in 11.1 seconds.

Sample price: 1.8 Softback in 1998 – £16,570.

Number built: 505,957.

◀ With the 1997 Freelander, Land Rover was, finally, ahead of the curve, becoming the first European manufacturer with a small SUV to combat the mounting Japanese incursion.

jockeying to formulate a 'lifestyle' off-roader. Land Rover's 'Pathfinder' concept won the day, although it was imperative that it would use engines (the aluminium K Series) shared with Rover cars. Fortunately, BMW's deep pockets enabled the British firm to accelerate development at just the right moment.

▶ The weirdly-named Softback was perhaps the more radical of the Freelanders, with its fold-down rear hood and glass roof bestowing something of a beach buggy touch.

▶▶ Land Rover's novel Hill Descent Control system gave sure-footed four-wheel drive coordination in the Freelander – this is the five-door estate – without the need for a hefty transfer box.

Here was a brand new monocoque design, the first Landie without a separate chassis, offered as either an upright five-door estate or a decidedly funky two-door convertible with optional hard-top.

The clanking mechanism of a two-speed transfer box to give four-wheel drive was replaced by a front-mounted Intermediate Reduction Drive and a viscous coupling unit in the drive shaft to the rear axle; downhill control to coordinate was afforded by an electronic 'Hill Descent Control' employing the foundation ABS braking system to limit the Freelander's speed. It was a permanent four-wheel drive system, and there were no low-range ratios nor any locking differential, so it was never going to be the choice of the Paras or Scottish hill farmers; yet decent off-road traction in line with the Freelander's leisure aspirations was there in abundance.

The man in charge of the new car's looks, Gerry McGovern, said at the time: 'Every feature should do a job while conveying what the vehicle can do. Land Rovers have to be robust, solid, go-anywhere. Vehicles like these have to be usable. With most road cars, sure, they're styled. But working at Land Rover allows us to be, almost, industrial designers.' The overall effect was entirely new but elements of the continuum included the 'clam-shell' bonnet, allowing easy engine access, the castellations on the

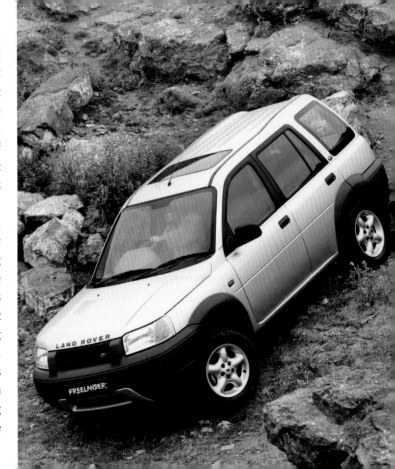

bonnet top making the Freelander easy to position on the road, and the equal glass-to-bodywork relationship that makes Land Rovers appear lofty yet balanced.

The Freelander was another big hit, becoming Europe's best-selling compact SUV almost instantly. And what it proved was that car buyers were drawn to a commanding driving position, the security of four-wheel drive for on- and occasional off-road driving, a rugged stance and a versatile interior. All of them, of course, tenets of every Land Rover so far, but the Freelander could easily do without the sort of raw capability that would allow it to cleave through jungle or assist a coastguard or tree surgeon. This trend helped to influence the Discovery II, launched in 1998.

Under its familiar but thoroughly reworked body (every panel bar the rear door was altered) the locking centre differential was disconnected and permanent four-wheel drive was provided, Freelander-style, by a clever combination of traction control and Land Rover's Hill Descent Control. The locking diff could be easily hooked up but virtually no-one chose to do so. It was deleted entirely in 2001 but returned, as an extra-cost option, three years later, Land Rover anxious lest its omission led to any accusations that the cars were going soft . . .

Disco II used the original's 100in wheelbase but with a body extended at the back so the two extra passenger seats could be normal, forward-facing fixtures. An optional self-levelling rear suspension set-up, featuring air springs, furnished excellent ride quality for those rearmost occupants – indeed, Europe-bound seven-seaters had this as standard. The tidy-looking new frontage housed more changes, as the V8 engine was now an enlarged 4-litre and the turbodiesel was a brand new

five-cylinder, the Td5, with a computer-controlled electronic fuel-injection system and a centrifugal oil filter to extend service intervals.

Simultaneously, this new engine arrived in the venerable Defender to make it the most responsive traditional diesel Land Rover so far. It powered all Defenders including an interesting new model introduced in June 2000, a four-door 110 Double Cab featuring the two front rows of a Station Wagon's seats but with a 1035mm-long open pick-up back that could carry more than a tonne in payload.

A major overhaul came to the Discovery in 1998 with the Disco II. The wheelbase was the same but almost every body panel was changed and the rear was lengthened to provide for seven forward-facing seats.

Did you know?

Camper conversion specialists Dormobile added a Land Rover to its catalogue in the early 1960s, complete with rising roof, beds and miniature kitchen. But many owners preferred the more expensive Carawagon conversion done by Searle of Sunbury-on-Thames, with a permanent, domed roof extension.

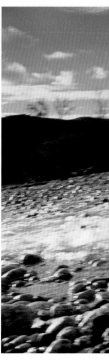

▲ Range Rover Mark III and the old charisma is back thanks to the detailed attention of temporary Land Rover custodian BMW; the car was launched to great acclaim in 2000.

▲ Traction control and Hill Descent Control combined to electronically control the Discovery II's four-wheel drive, sidelining the transfer box – not that many owners noticed, or cared.

THIRD-GENERATION RANGE ROVER

The third iteration of Range Rover was one of the great things achieved during BMW's short and turbulent ownership of Rover and Land Rover from 1994 until 2000. It cost £1bn to develop, making it the most important project for the British motor industry in 2000.

The dashing style was back in abundance, the luxury and interior ambience were awesomely accomplished, while a stiff monocoque body construction with interconnected air-sprung independent suspension all round – replacing the separate chassis frame and rigid axles – made it feel exceptionally nimble off-road. The initial BMW V8 engines were later replaced with Jaguar V8s to wholly reinstate that special Range Rover facet: Britishness!

The third incarnation of Range Rover arrived in 2001, and its smooth new styling led to corresponding facelifts for the Discovery and Freelander (now offered with 2-litre BMW diesel and 2.5 V6 Rover petrol power) in 2002. As something of a consolation prize, the Defender received a new dashboard. But all this was window-dressing next to the 2004 announcement of the totally new Discovery.

Land Rover called its new styling 'uncompromising', some thought it slabby, but there was no mistaking it for anything else with its vast expanses of flat panels, big semi-circular wheelarches, and general image of being hewn from solid metal. Actually, quite a lot of the original Discovery's features were carried over, notably the stepped roofline and the asymmetrical rear screen, but the extended wheelbase – so access to the third row of seats was easy – made it seem much more substantial.

The all-new engine line-up was led by a new 2.7-litre V6 turbodiesel, the TdV6, sourced from Ford's Dagenham factory and co-designed with Peugeot, but also included a beefy 4.4-litre V8 furnished by Jaguar. In the technical department, Land Rover was slowly relinquishing its traditional Forth Bridge construction methods for better fuel

▼ A 2001 facelift brought a refreshed visage to Freelander, shown, and Discovery to bring them into line stylistically with the Range Rover.

▲ The sumptuous new interior of the Discovery 3 boasted so-called 'stadium seating' so that all the seven occupants could have a great view of the terrain.

◄ The Discovery 3 was a radical departure for Land Rover, introducing an all-new monocoque body riding on a ladder-frame chassis and cradling the four-wheel drive and suspension units.

economy and on-road handling (although not weight, as the new Disco was heavier than its predecessor). It featured the main engine bay and passenger compartment as a monocoque but a separate ladder frame chassis for the four-wheel drive transmission and the independent coil-sprung air suspension with adjustable cross-linked settings.

Hill Descent Control plus traction and stability control packages were all standard. Something new was Terrain Response – selectable modes of four-wheel drive where the transmission automatically adjusts to the anticipated conditions. Drivers didn't need to worry overmuch about their off-road driving skills; they just chose 'Sand', 'Grass, Gravel & Snow', 'Mud & Ruts' or 'Rock Crawl' via a dial on the dashboard and gearbox settings, suspension height, differential lock and throttle response were all electronically adjusted to suit. Rock Crawl, for example, extended the suspension to its limits, gave the wheels maximum articulation, locked the differentials and advised the driver to switch to Low Range.

It made the Discovery 3 an SUV for everyman, much as its trendy image and high price tended to make it a rare sight in farmyards.

It was a lot of car and, perhaps predictably, so much new technology in one mighty package gave early Discovery 3s built in

▲ The Discovery 3 was a handsome beast in a hewn-from-solid sort of way, and proved immensely popular, although it was probably a bit too fancy – and costly – as an everyday farm hack.

◄ Terrain Response was a new 'dial-up' system of pre-set four-wheel drive modes for the Discovery 3 – would you go for 'Mud & Ruts' or 'Rock Crawl' in this situation?

Did you know?

In May 2011, Tata Motors began assembling the Freelander II at a new plant in Pune, India, working with complete kits of parts dispatched from Land Rover's factory at Halewood on Merseyside. It resulted in a 40 per cent drop in local prices over the heavily taxed imported built-up equivalent.

FACTS & DATA: LAND ROVER DISCOVERY 3/4
(aka LR3/LR4)

On sale: 2004–.

Engine capacity, configuration: 2720–2993cc, V6 turbodiesel; 4009cc, V6 petrol (US market only); 4394-4999cc, V8 petrol.

Bodystyles: five-door, five/seven-seater station wagon.

Dimensions: 4838–4849mm long, 1841–1892mm high, 1915–2022mm wide; wheelbase 2885mm.

Top speed: from 112–121mph.

Sample acceleration figures: 2720cc TDV6 – 0–60mph in 11 seconds; 4993cc V8 LR4 – 0–60mph in 7.9 seconds.

Sample prices: Discovery 3 2.7 TDV6 in 2006 – £43,540; Discovery 4 5.0 HSE in 2012 – £51,195.

Number built: 372,600 approx to autumn 2012.

The asymmetric shape of the rear screen was continued on the Discovery 3, repeating the cue of the stepped roofline.

generation Freelander, a car that would be the first Land Rover to be built in Britain away from the Solihull headquarters. With anticipated demand set to soar, space had been found for it on the production lines at the former Ford plant at Halewood on Merseyside, alongside the Jaguar X-Type.

Solihull a reputation for patchy reliability. Land Rover was forced to mount an all-out assault on quality control and customer satisfaction. At the same time, it was putting the finishing touches to the second-

A Discovery 3 well on its way to completion on the Solihull production line – both car and plant being totems of the British motor industry's ability, still, to compete with the world's best.

The Freelander II of 2006 was a slightly bigger and considerably roomier improvement over the original, keeping the character but vastly boosting its appeal in terms of slick interior design and finish. Ground clearance was raised. The old Rover KV6 was gone, replaced by a Ford-sourced, Volvo-designed 3.2-litre straight-six mounted transversely, while the 2.2-litre turbodiesel came from yet another joint venture, this time with Peugeot. Basically front-wheel drive cars, the new Freelander achieved four-wheel drive using a novel pre-charged, electronically-controlled coupling made by Swedish company Haldex, to give instant response, allied to Land Rover's superb and much-vaunted (it scooped a Queen's Award for Innovation) Terrain Response.

➤ A total rethink underpinned the Freelander II, making for a bigger overall vehicle with a better quality interior and a transverse 3.2-litre Volvo straight-six petrol engine as standard.

➤ In March 2009, the Freelander 2 TD4_e became the world's first SUV with an intelligent stop/start system to cut pollution in city traffic.

Did you know?

The SVX was a wild one-off Defender 90 shown at the 1999 Frankfurt motor show. It featured open bodywork with substantial roll cage, huge 20in custom wheels, Recaro racing seats and cast alloy gearlever knobs. Nine years later, a version of the SVX went on sale to mark Land Rover's 60th anniversary. It was launched by Zara Phillips at the Red Cross Ball and each vehicle had a unique numbered plaque.

➤ Zara Phillips did the 60th anniversary honours for Land Rover at the 2009 British Red Cross Ball, by unveiling the celebratory SVX special-edition Defender.

In 2009, the Discovery was thoroughly worked over to turn it from the 3 to the 4; here is the revised car making light work of towing an aluminium-bodied, American-made Airstream caravan.

FACTS & DATA: LAND ROVER FREELANDER II (aka LR2)

On sale: 2006–.

Engine capacity, configuration: 3192cc straight-six cylinder petrol; 2179cc straight-four cylinder turbodiesel.

Bodystyles: five-door, five-seater station wagon.

Dimensions: 4501mm long, 1740mm high, 1910mm wide; wheelbase 2659mm.

Top speed: from 118–124mph.

Sample acceleration figures: 3192cc – 0–60mph in 8.4 seconds; 2179cc – 0–60mph in 8.7 seconds.

Sample price: Td4 HSE in 2006 – £30,935.

Number built: 349,000 approx to autumn 2012.

In June 2008, Land Rover changed hands. Ford had owned it since 2000, confident it had picked a gem from the wreckage of Rover Group broken up by BMW, and adding it to great marques like Aston Martin, Jaguar, Lincoln and Volvo in its Premier Automotive division. But most of the car industry mega-mergers of the 1990s and early new

millennium unravelled in the mid-2000s as bosses were sternly reminded to build solid profits rather than inflated egos and Byzantine empires. Apart from Toyota and its home-grown Lexus, the biggest mass-producers mostly proved themselves terrible at running smaller, prestige marques; and as BMW found with Rover and Mercedes-Benz with Chrysler, upmarket brands were no better at inhabiting the mass-market mindset.

So Ford sold Land Rover and Jaguar together for $2.3bn to Tata, the Indian conglomerate involved in everything from teabags to sheet steel. The two marques were drawn together again as they had been in 1968 with the formation of British Leyland. Only, this time, the prospects looked so much more promising for the newly formed Jaguar-Land Rover (JLR).

Subsequently the new management, now able to control Land Rover's destiny, has shown no let-up in the constant fettling of its entire line-up. In 2009, for instance, the Discovery was thoroughly rejuvenated with new detail styling inside and out, and its engines uprated to a 3-litre TDV6 and a 5-litre petrol V8; an emissions-cutting e-Technologies package included Intelligent Power System Management where the alternator only charges the battery at the most economical moment, and a lowered engine idle speed. An example of this latest iteration became, in 2012, the one-millionth Discovery to be sold, a white-painted, Russian-specification car that left the factory and embarked on an 8000-mile drive to Beijing, raising money for the Red Cross to fund humanitarian projects in Uganda.

The last few years have seen Land Rover focus on the new Range Rover Sport, the wildly successful Range Rover Evoque, and now a brand new Range Rover flagship. But what of that trusty old warhorse, the Defender?

The year 2006 saw a raft of changes. Many of them made the Defender more user-friendly, such as the first totally redesigned fascia since the Series III of 1971 and a modern heating and ventilation system to boost demisting and general

◄ A Defender SVX in reflective mood as it pauses on a deserted beach to ponder 60 years as the much-quoted 'Best 4x4xFar'.

◄ In 2006 this totally redesigned dashboard appeared in all new Defenders, a vast improvement on its previously higgledy-piggledy signal-box controls.

▲ The stretched crew-cab pick-up option arrived in 1985 (this is a 2006-era Defender), 17 inches longer to give a 127in wheelbase; it became the 130 five years later, simply to neaten up the model numbering system!

interior comfort. But the majority of the modifications were designed to keep the ageing vehicle compliant with ever-stricter vehicle legislation. The Td5 engine – the last built by Land Rover in-house at Solihull – was replaced with a 2.4-litre Duratorq turbodiesel as used in the Ford Transit but specially adapted for off-road use. It offered the same power, a wider spread of torque, better fuel consumption but, mostly, cleaner emissions. There was a new six-speed gearbox and an improved, quieter transfer box.

Inside, 'type approval' safety laws had made their mark. Station wagon models saw the old-fashioned and patently more

◀ The Range Rover Sport united the Discovery 3 platform with customised Range Rover styling to produce a performance-focused 4x4 sports saloon – another instant winner.

▲ Land Rover's major Defender upgrade in 2006 also included this prominent bonnet bulge, needed to accommodate the newly-specified Ford Duratorq 2.4-litre turbodiesel engine.

➤ In 2007, staff in the Solihull tool room built this full-size replica of the Land Rover model featured in Aardman Animation's cartoon series *Shaun the Sheep*. To recreate it, they used a 1951 Series I chassis and panels from several later vehicles; it worked, passed its MoT, and set off on a promotional tour for the show.

▲ You can clearly see how the excellent approach and departure angles of a Defender 90 – made possible by high ground clearance and short front and rear bodywork overhangs – give it a huge off-road advantage over more elaborate modern rivals.

dangerous side-facing seats at the back replaced with normal, forward-facing ones. This would make the three-door 90 a four-seater (down from six) and the 110 five-door a seven-seater (down from nine). An addition to the range was a new Utility bodystyle, a five-seater version of the 110 with the third rear side windows blanked out – and no rearmost seats – to form a hybrid van/personnel carrier. For taxation purposes, this version was reclassified as a pure commercial vehicle in 2009, hugely boosting its appeal to business.

The bonnet acquired a bulge so that the engine could be positioned to allow deformable space in the event of

▲ This Station Wagon Utility bodystyle was added to the range in 2006, making for a five-seater hybrid van that three years later was re-classed for tax purposes as a commercial vehicle, hugely boosting its appeal.

▲ Yet another body configuration for the Defender is this 110 crew-cab pick-up, an option that had been under consideration for years but only went on sale in 2001.

a pedestrian impact. All laudable stuff, of course. The only real pity was that the well-liked ventilation flaps under the windscreen had to go to accommodate the new dashboard.

With twenty-first-century sales still running at around 20–25,000 a year, the Defender continued to find a ready market, each year adding to its status as a gold-plated classic legend. The years, though, are catching up with it. In 2012 came another engine change to keep the Defender within the legal 'Euro V' pollution limits. At 2.2 litres, it was a smaller capacity four-cylinder

unit, but offering barely altered power and torque outputs thanks to its better efficiency. A particulate filter fixed close to the exhaust manifold helped regenerative cleaning; and it was much quieter.

With this latest Defender came an unspoken admission from Land Rover that this bout of fettling would be the vehicle's last. Regulations slated for introduction in 2015 require every vehicle on sale,

Fashions may come and go but when it comes to getting through harsh weather conditions on inhospitable roads, there's still little to touch a Land Rover Defender.

commercials included, to incorporate airbags, and to meet significant new standards in pedestrian impact protection. There is no chance the venerable Defender can satisfy either of these mandates, nor the upcoming Euro VI emissions limits. Indeed, even some existing Defenders are becoming a liability to their owners, after several insurance companies declared in 2012 they would henceforth refuse cover on pre-2007 station wagons with sideways-facing passenger bench seats.

114

◄ Land Rover and lithium ion battery company Axeon co-created this all-electric Defender in 2011, for unobtrusive use in unspoilt South African safari parks.

◄◄ The expedition-style Safety Devices roof rack on this Defender 110 station wagon was essential for the annual charity fund-raising G4 Challenge events from 2003–9, as was the exhaust stove pipe . . .

The only way for the Defender to comply with modern standards would be for it to undergo a ground-up redesign. Fortunately for fans of the real Land Rover deal, that's exactly what is happening. A pointer to the vehicle's possible future form was presented at the 2011 Frankfurt Motor Show as the DC100 concept. Land Rover called it: 'The beginning of a four-year journey to design a relevant Defender for the 21st century'. The three-door hardtop (there was a DC100 Sport open show car

too) sported three-abreast front seats with folding rear passenger seats to increase load carrying capacity. Body panels were made of natural, recyclable material, the seat cushions from castor oil. Fancy new technology included Terrain i-Scanning, 'Always On' communication telematics, integral induction charging centres, and a multi-functional touchscreen sat-nav unit that was removable and portable. The four-wheel drive system sported so-called Torque Vectoring for maximum traction, disconnectable four-wheel drive for on-road cruising, and an eight-speed ZF gearbox. It's thought the final vehicle will use a full-frame chassis with the body bonded on top.

The most tangible part of the concept car of all was its engine, an all-new, low-emission 2-litre four-cylinder petrol/diesel series designed in-house by Jaguar Land Rover and scheduled for production in a brand new, £355m West Midlands engine plant.

Only, when the 'new' Defender arrives in 2015, it will be as an import to Britain. The new utility vehicle looks likely to be built in India, probably at Pune, at numbers as high as 40,000 annually; this is to keep costs low, making the new vehicle an attractive prospect in emerging markets. This will also free up space in Solihull and Halewood for more of Land Rover's other, high-value cars, although 'New Defenders' could be assembled in the UK from Indian-supplied kits for European markets.

The old Defender, incidentally, is not dead yet. Not by a country mile. Pure commercial 110 and 130 versions seem likely to live on even after 2015, assuming the rules can be bent or, well, eased back, a little. Could it be that the classic, brilliant Land Rover will just make it across the increasingly hostile terrain of its seventh full decade before its long-feared demise? Not much has got in its way so far, so why not?

◀ In 2010 Arthur Goddard, who led the engineering development team for the original Land Rover in 1947, was reunited with his 'baby'; the 89-year-old flew in from Australia to retrace his test route for the vehicle, shown here crossing Packington Ford, Warwickshire.

➤ The compact Range Rover Evoque has proved wildly successful, with 88,000 cars sold in less than 12 months and a slew of top awards under its belt.

➤➤ The three- and five-door versions of the Range Rover Evoque are built alongside the Land Rover Freelander II at Halewood on Merseyside, which is working round the clock to meet massive global demand.

◀ The country comes to town; a cool, urban look for the Defender X-Tech limited edition hardtop, which briefly joined the range in 2011.

▶ The 2012 Land Rover Defender 110 Station Wagon in mean and moody action, with an all-British appeal that is as strong as ever.

▶ Yet another new diesel engine, this time a 2.2-litre, arrived for the Defender in 2012, the new unit helping the ageing vehicle keep pace with ever-tougher emissions laws.

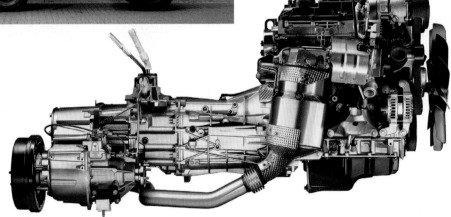

▲ The DC100 concept is the strongest hint yet as to where an all-new Defender might be heading, although we can be pretty certain it will be built abroad to save costs, probably in India.

➤ DC100 features disconnectable four-wheel drive for when this kind of tenacious off-road performance is not required, but ambling along the Fulham Road is.

➤ The Defender just keeps bowling along, but its days are now numbered for sure as safety and emissions legislation is closing in on a design that, although much evolved, is 60 years old.

➤➤ Shallow rivers in the English countryside just seem to lay down a challenge to Land Rover owners . . . unless, of course, this is a flooded lane, which it might well be.

◀ The fourth-generation Range Rover was launched amid much fanfare in September 2012; would that we had the room to go into detail, but we thought we'd squeeze a picture in anyway, for the sake of completeness.

▲ Land Rover's ancient and modern showing at the 2008 Goodwood Festival of Speed ranged from the hallowed Series I original to the futuristic LRX concept . . . shortly to be made real as the Range Rover Evoque.

▶ The Defender waves goodbye with a particularly muddy mudflap.

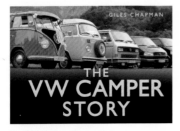

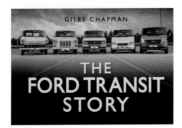